About the autho

Balkar Gill was born in England, the son of Indian
migrants from the Punjab, India. He currently
lives in Harborne and works in the city of
Birmingham as a Lecturer. He is married and has
a young daughter. He has a BA degree in Political
Economy and an MSc in International Politics
from Bristol University.

He is the author of a number of previous
sociological articles published in the Sociology
Review Journal.

Email: balgillrowley@yahoo.com

A MODERN GUIDE TO: ARRANGING YOUR OWN MARRIAGE

BALKAR GILL

For Vandana, Saffy,
Mum, Dad and John

Contents

Introduction

The popular stereotype of most Asians in Britain having arranged marriages is about as outdated as the notion that all corner shop owners are Asian or that all Muslims are potential terrorists. Both notions, despite being popularised by the media, do not reflect the social reality. Such views tend to relate to a very small minority and more often than not tend to result in popular misconceptions.

There has been a dramatic cultural shift in the last decade amongst the Asian community in Britain, such that rather than having 'arranged marriages' thrust upon them by parents and extended family, Asians are now 'arranging their own marriages'. The explosion and popularity of Indian matrimonial websites such as Shaadi.com epitomising such a sea change in cultural traditions. Parents are now taking a back seat in the whole marriage process, whereas in the past they played a central role in selecting their children's life partner. Third generation British Asians are navigating a middle route not only between the wishes and aspirations of their parents but also the traditions of their Eastern and Western cultures.

This book aims to provide a guide to the key factors and issues that may shape the decision making process when selecting a life partner within the British Asian community. Despite the fact that young Asians are increasingly taking their destinies into their own hands, traditional considerations such as caste, colour, ethnicity, family background and occupation continue to play a vital role in the decision making process.

Part of my aim is to identify who and what constitutes a so-called 'suitable partner' for young Asians arranging their own marriages and how such considerations reflect on the Asian community in Britain as a whole.

You will discover that the idea of romantic love as understood in the West (and championed by the Bollywood film industry) tends to figure lowly in the Asian marriage merry go round. This perhaps would be of no surprise to Tina Turner when she sang: "What's love got to do, got to do, got to do with it....."

Balkar Gill

Is he a doctor or a dentist?

Stereotypes often become stereotypes because they tend to be rooted in some generalised truth based on fact or experience. How often have you met an Accountant that is boring; a female that doesn't like to shop or a Premiership footballer that has a high IQ? The Asian community, like any other, lives up to its fair share of stereotypes, most notably in relation to occupational choice. Labour market surveys show that Asians in Britain are over represented in a number of professions, namely that of Doctors (10 times the national average) , Dentists, Lawyers, Pharmacists and Accountants (the latter, for those of a boring disposition of course). The more popular stereotype of Asian taxi drivers and corner shop owners still applies, although in terms of the latter they are an increasingly dying breed with companies like Tesco and Sainsbury's developing their 'Local' mini-supermarket brands.

The obsession with occupation is most apparent when it comes to issues of marriage in the Asian community. An individual's professional background is a key factor in determining marriage suitability. Asian parents are commonly associated with having a pathological preoccupation with their children marrying someone with a good job. Of course, every parent regardless of ethnic background wants their child to marry a well-to-do educated person but Asians go beyond this aspiration such that it becomes an obsession and very much part of the cultural landscape.

When potential matches are identified for their children the first question Asian parents ask is 'what does he do?' This question is usually quickly followed by others relating to the potential suitors family background – is he the right caste? Height – is he tall? Skin colour - is he fair? However, if the potential match scores highly on the first question, the answers to the last three tend to become irrelevant. Thus, a short, dark, rotund, overweight and unattractive insular Doctor is much preferred to a tall, muscular, handsome, light skinned, affable car mechanic.

The importance of occupational background was highlighted at a recent family function. A young cousin decided to tell her parents that she had met someone that she would like to settle down with. The conversation, reminiscent of a Monty Python sketch, went something along the following lines:

Cousin: 'Mom, Dad I've met someone'.
Mother: 'Ok, that's great beta, who is it and what does he do?'
Cousin: 'I've known him for two years now.'
Father: 'Okay, good. What does he do?'

Cousin: 'We get on really well and he makes me so happy.'
Mother: 'That's good, but what is his job'.
Cousin: 'I hope you'll both be happy for me.'
Mother: 'I'm sure dear, what does he do for a living?'
Cousin: 'He's really talented and works really hard'.
Father: 'Very good, very good but what is it that he does?'
Cousin: 'He's an artist, a sculptor.'
Parents: 'Oh......' (deep sigh by both parents followed by a lot of head shaking and sombre looks as if someone had just died!)

So if a sculptor is not the preferred parental choice, what is? Or if you are arranging your own marriage what occupation should you go for?

Top of the occupational league table, not surprisingly are those jobs that are associated with the highest incomes. Company Directors and Chief Executives being top of the tree closely followed by Financial Managers According to data from the Office of National Statistics the average annual income for Financial Managers being £72,124 for the 187,000 or so in Britain today. Accountants may be boring but spending their money may be one way of offsetting that flaw and making married life more bearable.

Medical practitioners take third place. The average annual income being £67,895 for the

84,000 or so Doctors in Britain. This average, as with any average can be deceptive. For example, if we were to separate out hospital consultants, the average basic pay rises to around £94,000 per year (this figure ignores income from private work). Self employed GPs (holding NHS contracts) can earn in the region of £80,000 to £120,000 per year. Some would argue that such high income rates helps explain why the NHS is drained of resources, its all going to the Doctors and Surgeons.

Within the Asian culture Doctors are held in particularly high esteem and the occupation is seen as highly respectable. This in a community where respect or izzat is as important to Asians as it is to a Mafia don and his crime family. Such respect accorded to the medical profession is linked to the perceived higher level of educational attainment which is also highly valued by Indians. Indeed, long before Tony Blair coined the slogan 'education, education, education' at a Labour Party conference, Asian parents across Britain could be heard saying the same thing to their children at teatime as they tucked into their aloo gobi and roti. Perhaps not surprisingly then government statistics reflect the fact that Indians (more specifically Hindus and Sikhs) are one of the highest performing ethnic groups in education in Britain today – second only to Chinese students.

Girls tend to do better than boys at most stages of education including SATs, GCSEs and A levels. This may be a reflection of the fact that Asian girls are often told (or threatened) that if they don't get a good education they will be married off at an early age. Such threats tend to act as a great motivator for girls to do well at school and go on to university thus delaying if not avoiding family pressure to get married. Indeed for many Asians in Britain university choice is often dictated not by academic reputation but by distance. That is, the university offering the greatest distance from home with the worst rail and road routes is the preferred option – surprise parental visits are thus rare and coming back home for the weekend minimised. Parents will often ask the children as to why they couldn't pick a closer university to which the stock response is: 'they don't offer the course I want to do'.

The popularity of Doctors as perfect partner material has no doubt been enhanced by programmes such as Casualty and Holby City. A female friend recently confided that when she dreams of her perfect wedding day, an Asian version of George Clooney's character in ER appears in the Sikh temple where the wedding ceremony takes place. The Asian George looking resplendent in a white turban and doctors white coat with a stethoscope around his neck instead of the traditional Indian flowery garlands.

Despite the glamour and income associated with the medical profession which has contributed to the notion that doctors constitute perfect marriage material. A couple of factors perhaps need to be taken into consideration. Firstly, doctors have one of the highest suicide rates amongst the professions – they are twice as likely to kill themselves compared with people working in other professions. Overwork, stress and easy access to drugs being some of the reasons for such a high suicide rate. Secondly, doctors are often accused of having 'god complexes' by virtue of being able to save lives. This often manifests itself in a feeling of superiority and arrogance which are not the most attractive features in a life partner.

Sheetal, a 32 year old Hindu divorcee from Leeds reflected on how when she married a Doctor in a semi – arranged marriage (that is, she had been introduced to her partner via family and they went on a number of 'dates' before committing to marriage) things started off well: 'He ticked all the boxes – educated, a doctor and the same ethnicity. Our married life started well but it soon became apparent that he saw himself as superior to me and most of my friends primarily because he was a Doctor. I am graphic designer and most of my friends are in the media industry – he often made derogative remarks and always seemed to look down his nose at us. He was also very controlling and thought he was always right. From that experience I have learnt that it is not what someone does for a living that is important....'

Dentists also enjoy a strong position in the preferred marriage partner stakes. However, with an average income of around £42,000 per annum, dentists are seen as the poor relations to doctors.

The typical starting salary being £27,500 (remember that those in private practice can earn significantly higher amounts and Dentist's with their own practices can earn significantly above the national averages).

Such inferiority is not restricted to income but extends to the notion that dentistry degrees are the easy or cop out option compared to degrees in medicine. Having said that, dentists are on a par with doctors in the suicide stakes with a higher than average rate for the professions. Researcher Steven Stacks suggested that this was a reflection of the fact that dentists suffer from relatively low status within the medical profession and tend to have strained relationships with their clients. This is not particularly surprising as few people look forward to visiting the dentist and having teeth extracted. Moreover, dentists are rarely thanked for the service they provide; again this is hardly surprising considering how much they charge – English dentists having the highest rates in Europe. Perhaps the old saying of 'paying through the nose should be changed to 'paying through the mouth'. Visits to the dentist being more financially rather than physically painful.

Asian dentists and doctors may be over – represented in the medical professions yet appear to be under-represented in the suicide statistics. White males taking pole position. So if you were thinking of bagging an Asian doctor or dentist as a husband / wife with a view to cashing on the life insurance policy, think again. Vets have an even higher suicide rate – nearly four times the national average and double that of doctors and dentists. Again stress and easy access to drugs have been cited as key factors. In terms of marriage options, Asian vets in the UK are in the extreme minority.

Lawyers also rank highly in the Asian culture as good strong marriage material. It is not uncommon to hear Asian parents at social events proudly stating that their son or daughter is doing law resulting in wistful sighs and nods of approval from other parents. The more cynical parent can be heard whispering to the person next to them that 'the son is more likely to be breaking the law rather than studying it!'

There are around 62,000 solicitors, lawyers, barristers and judges in Great Britain. The average income enjoyed by this group being approximately £49,970, however as mentioned earlier such statistics can be very deceptive. For example, only a very small handful of lawyers who work for the top law firms take home over £1 million per year which in turn skews the average income figure. At the other end of the spectrum newly qualified solicitors can only expect to earn on average up to £25,000. Indeed some partners in small high street firms cannot expect to earn much more if the firm is not particularly profitable.

It is perhaps a common misperception that the job of a solicitor is relatively well paid. Rather for the majority, the opposite is the case such that pipe fitters in Britain have a higher average income of £28, 253. Moreover, the glamour associated with legal work (no doubt fuelled by popular tv programmes such as LA law and Ally McBeal) masks the reality of boring mundane work. As one lawyer friend commented when asked what she does: 'I go through document after document crossing the t's and and putting dots on the i's. Sometimes I get to put in capitals!' She went on to explain how she has to account for almost every minute of the day, such as itemising how long she spends on a phone call or composing a letter. She then lamented how she might be better of in manual work: 'at least in factories people only have to clock on and off once in the day. I have to account for my every move – I'm sure they'll want be to itemise my toilet time next!'

Research conducted in America suggests that lawyers are amongst the most unhappy and unhealthy of the professions. It has been estimated that one in three lawyers suffer from clinical depression, alcoholism or drug abuse. Now this maybe an essential characteristic for success for our pop stars if the likes of Amy Winehouse and Britney Spears is anything to go by, however perhaps not for the upholders of the law of the land. One group of researchers found that the rate of alcoholism among lawyers is double that of adults generally. Other research estimated that

26% of lawyers had used cocaine at least once, twice the rate of the general population. Not surprisingly divorce rates appear to be higher amongst lawyers when compared to other professions.

Despite the reality, the legal profession continue to enjoy a valued position within the Asian community closely followed by teachers. Higher education teachers, of which there are around 87, 000 earn on average £37,678 per year. For the 308, 000 secondary teachers in Britain the average is £31,520. The status accorded to teachers can be located in the fact that education is a highly valued commodity within the Asian culture. This reflects the fact that for most first generation Asians in Britain education was a luxury. In places such as India, Bangladesh and Pakistan education was costly and thus often limited to a wealthy minority. Teachers in these countries also enjoyed a high status and tended to rule their classrooms with an iron grip and often an iron rod! Corporal punishment was the norm whereby misbehaviour, even on the smallest scale, was not tolerated. Punishment at school not only brought shame on the individual but also on the family, such that there would be more punishment at home. Indeed, with a growth of the ASBO culture in Britain and a perception of an increasingly violent youth some would argue that our education system should mirror that of the Indian subcontinent.

Whilst not hitting the high income rates of surgeons and bankers, teachers are attractive marriage material apart from being part of a culturally acceptable profession. The long holiday's teachers get, which can be up to three months a year, mean that they can make great contributions to childcare. Long summer holidays and numerous half terms (not to mention various days off for 'staff development' otherwise known as 'staff doss days') mean that your partner is around to look after the kids and thus reduce the financial burden of increasingly extortionate childcare costs – the average cost of a fulltime nursery place being £159.00 per week. Also, as they are part of the teaching profession one would hope that they may contribute to the education of your little loved ones.

Doctors, dentists, lawyers, accountants and teachers have consistently topped the occupational league table when it comes to picking the perfect marriage partner within the Asian community. This preference is shared by those of Pakistani, Bangladeshi, Sri Lankan or Indian origin. The obsession with income is the most obvious common denominator, however crucially; such occupations are seen as 'respectable'. Whereas professions centred on the world of arts and culture tend to be dismissed. Tell your parents you intend to become a painter, actor or writer, the most likely response is 'don't be so stupid, this is not a profession, how will you make money?' This is usually followed by a swift smack around the head.

A successful 30 year old Indian artist friend reflected on the night she informed her parents that she intended to pursue a career as an actress. Her father simply said:

'I do not want to hear such nonsense in my house again!'

He walked away in disgust heading for the drinks cabinet and the bottle of Johnny Walker whiskey (an essential in any Sikh household!). Whereas the mothers response was a little more dramatic. A response that would not look out of place in a Bollywood movie. She fell to her knees, her hands reaching for her head, shrieking wildly:

'How will you ever be married! What shame you will bring on the family by doing this pornography. What shame!'

It was as if some great act of blasphemy had been committed. An ungodly act that would result in great suffering for all · the greatest sin of all, making yourself less marketable in the marriage merry-go-round. The artist friend did reflect that it may have been easier to come out of the closet and inform her parents that she was gay.

Artists and musicians on average earn around £23,000 per year and as already mentioned tend not to enjoy a favourable position in the marriage stakes. Such inequality becomes more pronounced when we look at the position of those at the other end of the occupational league table, namely the less skilled and manual professions. This group is most obviously excluded in most Asian matrimonial websites. Any cursory analysis of such sites quickly highlights the dominance of the non manual skilled professions. You would be hard pressed to find reference to a car mechanic, security guard, taxi driver, sewing machinist or telephonist. These professions appear to be almost invisible, which is a great shame considering the contribution such workers make to the running of the economy. Moreover, it is perhaps ironic that first generation Asian parents were often employed in such low paid sectors, yet they do not want their kids to marry into such occupations.

The focus on higher level professions has led to people lying about their professions on Indian dating sites. Zaiba (a 28 year old solicitor from Manchester) met a guy via one of the Asian matrimonial sites who said he was a trainee accountant at Heathrow BAA. They dated for a few months. One day, whilst waiting for her parents at Heathrow airport (Terminal 1) who were returning from a flight from India, she spotted the guy she was dating wearing what looked like a baggage handlers uniform. She confronted him there and then about his occupation to which he responded with anger and resentment: 'I said I was going to be an Accountant'. He did attempt to salvage the relationship later apologising for the deceit by stating he was too embarrassed to say he was a baggage handler. Zaiba decided not to pursue things on this occasion.

The average income for the 15,000 or so taxi drivers in Britain today is £15, 958, whereas the 24,000 sewing machinists can expect to earn around £12,502 per year. Sales and retail assistants do not fare much better earning on average £13,203 per year. Such workers exist on a wage significantly below the national average income which is approximately £25,000. The only saving grace for those who marry into such occupational groups is that factors such as love, passion and affection may play a more important role than income levels and job status.

In everyday conversations about marriage people often emphasize the importance of factors such as personality, intelligence, compatibility, sexual chemistry, passionately stating that what a person does and how much they earn are irrelevant. The reality is somewhat different and only the most honest admit to this fact. A highly successful female lawyer friend openly admits that she and her peer group would only consider professionals as marriage material. She confided that she had had affairs with Asian males from the lower ranked professions but saw these as 'a bit of fun'. She reflected on how she once dated a 'gorgeous Bollywood hunk' that was sweet, caring, down to earth and great father material. When asked what the problem was she responded: "He was a prison guard and probably earned a quarter of my salary. Although he was lovely to look at, he wasn't the brightest. I guess he was my bit of rough."

Go to any Asian wedding and it's a fair bet that most of the attractive married women are often accompanied by significantly less attractive men. Where the women are charismatic and beautiful the men are often unpleasant looking with dour personalities. One might suspect that they have hidden depths or a large manhood, however usually the only thing large about them is their pay packets. The common denominator is that such male partners have high paying jobs or come from wealthy families. Looks may not matter, but occupation and money certainly does.

Parental contributions

Despite the fact that 2nd and 3rd generation Asians are increasingly 'arranging their own marriages', parents still play a significant role in the process. Most obviously, parental consent and approval is still actively sought for a potential partner. Whilst in the dominant white British culture parents tend a take a back seat, Asian parents are up in the passenger seat pushing, if allowed, to get into the driving seat. It appears that although young British Asians are immersed in British culture and wholeheartedly lap up all that Western culture has to offer in terms of work, fashion, drinking, clubbing, dating and so on, when it comes to matters of marriage and introducing a life partner, parental permission is still needed. A high flying 36 year old male Hindu surgeon commented:

"Even though I moved away from home when I was 18 years old and lived a life of hedonistic excess and debauchery, I still feel I can only bring home a girl my parents would approve of. I am highly successful; I work at the cutting edge of surgery with a huge responsibility in trying to save people's lives, yet I can't shake the traditions of meeting my parent's traditional expectations. I don't know whether its guilt or a desire to please, but whenever I meet a potential lifetime partner I do stop and think, 'will mom and dad approve'. I know my parents expect me to marry someone of equal social standing so I am expected to marry a professional of some sort. If I didn't they would be disappointed."

Asians parents may have less control over partner selection but they still maintain a powerful influence, however this may not always constitute a negative. Parents can and often do, perform a positive role and act as an informal dating or introduction agency. That is, they network with other parents or members of their community at various places and social events looking for potential suitors for their respective children. At temples, mosques and mandir throughout Britain key information is exchanged - usually limited to age, occupation and height. Once a potential match has been agreed phone numbers and photos are exchanged between the matchmakers. These details are then passed onto to their respective children, who are 'actively encouraged', to put it mildly, to arrange a meeting. A 32 year old Muslim female dentist commented:

"My parents are on a desperate mission to get me married. Each time I come home at weekends my mom has a handbag full of photos of potential marriage partners. On the reverse side of the photo the information is always the same – written down is the age, occupation, height and a phone number. Mom harasses me until I agree to give the person a call. The last number she gave me she got off an Asian woman she met at a local bus stop!"

The desire of parents to introduce their children to a suitable boy or girl often results in quality assurance issues. That is, the information parents are given or 'interpret' may not always resemble the truth, particularly in relation to occupation. Such that someone described as a being an 'IT consultant in a bank' may well turn out to be a poorly paid data inputter for HSBC; a marketing executive may turn out to be a telesales worker; and a medical practitioner may turn out to be a sales assistant in a Pharmacy! Such exaggeration or (in some cases) bare faced lies one may expect in tabloid newspapers, are not always the fault of overzealous parents, but usually generated by the suitors themselves. Those on the market, not surprisingly, want to market themselves as much as possible. A 26 year old Sikh male from Birmingham admitted:

"I have exaggerated a little about my job and qualifications with my parents, but it was easy, they are a little clueless. I've told them that I've got degree. I did go to university but I dropped out after the first year of a foundation course and got a job in Nottingham. I tell them I'm in the Finance industry and work as a Financial Advisor. The truth is I do telesales as a temp trying to sell mortgages over the phone. I know it's wrong but once I meet someone I'm hoping they won't be that bothered with what I do and I'm hoping another decent job will come along soon anyway."

Conclusion

Occupation continues to be a key consideration within the Asian community in matters of marriage. Now this is very similar to any other community in Britain in that a person's class position still matters in a so-called classless British society. The key difference is that within the Asian community such issues are much more pronounced and obvious. Asians tend not to do subtlety well. Hence, factors such as personality, intelligence, compatibility, lust, love etc tend to be relegated in favour of issues related to occupation and caste when a person is undertaking the process of arranging their own marriage.

Caste no bar

Back in the glorious 1980's Margaret Thatcher told us that class no longer matters. It seems the Iron Lady's influence extended across the Atlantic to India where politicians in the lok sabha in Dehli also heralded a new era in which they asserted caste no longer matters. However, in Britain today the caste system appears to be alive and well. Indeed, it's a vital consideration in determining the suitability of a potential life partner. Pick the wrong caste and you yourself risk becoming an outcaste from your family and the wider community.

Despite the fact that in politically correct classrooms and dinner parties across Britain it is universally acknowledged that the caste system is about as anachronistic as Windows 97' to a 14 year old and as useful as Betamax videos, caste continues to play a big part in Asian society. Almost all Asian matrimonial websites and matrimonial newspapers in India and Britain have caste as an important category, usually located just after the skin colour category (a fair complexion being the preferred option of course!)

Brief history

The chances of finding two historians that have the same opinion on the exact origins of the caste system is about as likely as getting Simon Cowell and Louis Walsh to agree on the talents of an X factor contestant. However, if we were to cast our minds back (pardon the pun) there is some consensus that the caste system as we know it originated over 3000 years ago. In around 1500 BC it is suggested that a Turk derived group of nomadic warriors known as the Aryans (no relation to Hitler's master race) set up the structure in the Indian subcontinent.

This system was rooted in a rational rather than a spiritual organisation of people into different occupational groups. It was only some time later in the 16th Century that those great colonialists, the Portuguese (Portugal's position a colonialist was superseded by the British) labelled, albeit mistakenly, the organisational structure as the caste system. The word caste derives from the Latin casta which essentially means chaste or pure. This term is linked to the Hindu 'varna' which basically refers to the categorization of occupations and is actually non-hereditary. The insidious significance of caste was then a social construct, that is, created by a certain group of people at a particular moment in history – a human invention.

As with most things, the interpretation of events, structures or peoples actions changes according to time and place. For example, you may find it hard to believe but at one time the motorway system leading into and out of Birmingham (affectionately known as spaghetti junction) was once viewed as engineering marvel and a panacea for the city's traffic ills. Similarly, it becomes evident that over time the caste system has been reinterpreted and distorted to suit those in power or those with vested interests to create a divisive stratified system.

The caste system has been transformed from being a relatively simple system of occupational organisation to a rigid system of social stratification rooted in inequality. One where a person's essential identity, status or social standing in society was not only defined by their occupation, but more importantly, that this position was determined from birth. That is, caste was determined as being inherited and therefore cannot be changed – as permanent as a birth mark. It can be argued then, that the caste system as we understand it today is a bastardized and much more pervasive version of the original occupational classification developed thousands of years ago. Nevertheless the modernised version persists such that an Asian persons marriage prospects still appear to be largely determined by birth.

The caste system was effectively made illegal in India in 1949. Unfortunately, as with most laws, their creation rarely results in the act intended to be prohibited actually being prohibited. Laws' forbidding underage sex hasn't meant that kids under 16 don't still have sex; the 1970 Equal Pay Act hasn't resulted in the removal of sexual discrimination in the workplace with women in the UK still on average earning 20 per cent less than men in similar professions. The caste system is no exception, officially illegal but still prevalent within Indian society and amongst the Indian diaspora from Britain to Australia.

It is estimated that there are well over 3000 castes in India today. Despite regional differences each caste system operates on the basis of similar fundamentals. Hinduism being the forerunner, effectively establishing the blueprint of a rigid social hierarchy characterised by social exclusion and inequality. The table below provides a summarised version of a Hindu based caste system with Brahmins occupying the top position and Dalits being located at the bottom of the hierarchy:

Occupational links:

Brahmin   Priests, scholars, teachers

Kshatriya   Warriors, rulers, landowners

Vaishya   Traders, merchants, agriculturalists

| Shudras labourers | Manual workers – craft workers, |
| Dalits sweepers | Menial occupations – cleaners, |

Now apart from the obvious ethical considerations as to how morally unacceptable such a system is, it seems to me that if we were to apply the caste system to contemporary Britain we quickly come across some problems. Surely the status of plumbers should be above that of traders (shop keepers) – the former being about as easy to find as a four leaf clover. What of dentists – should they be seen as manual workers? And teachers – go into any inner city comprehensive school and you'll find that the status accorded to teachers by students is somewhere just below rats and only just above cockroaches.

Top of the tree then is the Brahmin caste and it is no great coincidence that this group is composed of holy leaders. What better way to maintain your power and dominance than to accord yourself the highest status and sell this as your birthright determined by the big guy in the sky. Who can argue with divine intervention, karma and kismet? Maybe Karl Marx had a point when he said religion is the opium of the people. Brahmins not only saw themselves as the superior caste but wrote the guidelines and thus the system is cast in stone. They were the minority literate class thus

33

able to dupe the illiterate majority into accepting the authority of the caste system. Brahmins were effectively segregated from the lower castes in most if not all social affairs. This strict separation of the castes (or rather people) had at its very heart the idea of superiority and inferiority, thus suggesting that all people are not equal in the eyes of the Lord.

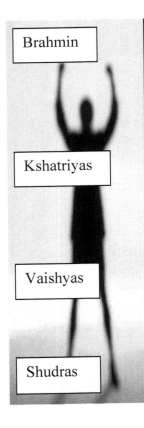

Brahmin

Kshatriyas

Vaishyas

Shudras

It is argued that the caste system reflects a deliberate misrepresentation of ancient Hindu manuscripts by religious scholars, resulting in a fraud that American Exxon executives would be proud of. Symbolic reference is made to Brahmins as the face of the lord or creator, Kshatriyas the arms, Vaishyas the thighs and Shudras the feet. But that is simply what it is, a symbolic reference. Nevertheless the religious scribes put a spin on the texts comparable to the deception by Alistair Campbell and the Labour Party when they said Saddam Hussein had weapons of mass destruction.

Those belonging to the bottom position have been party to a rebranding exercise. Dalit or 'the downtrodden' being the preferred term, replacing the previous label of 'untouchables'. This seems a pity as in American parlance the notion of being an untouchable has very different connotations, namely that of an elite crime fighting force epitomised by Mafiosi crime buster Eliot Ness in the movie 'The Untouchables'. Being untouchable was a badge of honour rather than a curse to be lived with.

The Dalit's were effectively seen as the outcastes of society. An unenviable position rooted in the notion that this group were regarded as polluted. Such pollution being linked to the type of work they undertook. The Dalit community has been traditionally associated with professions dealing with 'human emissions'. This eccentric use of the English language typical of Indians brought up during the Raj, refers to bodily discharges which smell a little more than car emissions although may not have as great an impact on climate change. Working with animals, dead and alive was also viewed as a polluting activity. It appears then that Vets in India perhaps did not enjoy the status of those in Britain and other so called Westernised countries.

The position of the untouchables was bad enough whereby any interaction with members of the higher caste Brahmins would result in the latter having to undergo a cleansing ceremony due to so-

35

called pollution. Yet a sub caste also existed, known as the 'unseeables'. This group were considered to be so polluted that they should not be seen at all. Thus the likelihood of a Brahmin using the old adage 'some of my best friends are untouchables...' wasn't such an issue. The notion of considering inter marriage didn't enter the realm of reality. Such a suggestion resulting in a reaction akin to the response of the clergy in the 15th Century when Columbus blasphemously dared to suggest the world was round not flat.

Not to be outdone by the Hindu's, other communities and groups have developed similar caste systems albeit with some variations. In the Northern part of India, namely the Punjab, Sikh's joined the bandwagon. Jatt's were traditionally seen as just below the Brahmins and Kshatriyas and thus part of the Vaiyshas caste. Mainly made up of farmers they constituted two thirds of the Sikh population in the Punjab.

However, over time and with growing prosperity in the villages, reflecting increasing crop yields, Jatts came to assume a position as important as Brahmins. City life in India may have been dominated by Brahmins, but in the villages and rural areas of the Punjab Jatts as landowners reigned supreme. More recently, with the exodus of many Sikhs to the West, it appears that Jatts have become self-appointed to the highest caste position. Whilst this may be historically dubious, to say the least, it again reflects the relative ease by which people reinterpret the past to suit themselves - read the memoirs of any politician for further evidence of this process.

The lower castes or Shudras are made up of, in order of perceived superiority: Ramgharias (tradesman or skilled workers undertaking building work for the higher castes); Darsi (tailors); Chimba (weavers); Halvyi (sweet makers); Chammar (leather workers); Lohaar (blacksmiths) and lastly the Churrah (cleaners) or untouchables. Other Punjabi sub castes do exist, such as Saini (poorer Jatts who rented rather than owned land), however to name them all would complicate an already confusing picture.

It is worth pointing out that caste is part of the Punjabi culture as opposed to the Sikh religion. The founding fathers of Sikhism identified equality as one of the central pillars of Sikhism. The founding father of Sikhism, Guru Nanak Dev Ji (1469 – 1538) stated that class, caste and status differences were mere social constructions and as a great social reformer Guru Nanak Dev Ji advocated the abolishment of the caste system. Incidentally, Guru Nanak Dev Ji was born into a Hindu family and his father was a Patwari (the equivalent to an Accountant) with a degree of social and political power so one could argue that Guru Nanak was born into a relatively privileged position and stood to benefit from the existing caste system.

The tenth Sikh guru, Guru Gobind Singh (1666 –
1708) effectively banned castes and asked all
followers of Sikhism to abandon their surnames
which effectively identified their caste positions.
These were to be replaced by Singh for males
meaning lions and Kaur for females meaning
princess, hence sweeping away with one effective
stroke the key indicators of a person's caste. Guru
Gobind Singh effectively enshrined this policy in
compiling the teachings of all the ten Gurus in the
Guru Granth Sahib or the Holy Scripture.
References to the idea of the equality of all people
can be found in the holy book such as 'Your Light
is the light in all beings, O creator (Guru Granth
Sahib, 1314) or '...there are no classes or castes in
the world hereafter...'(Guru Granth Sahib, 349).

Sikhism is a relatively young religion having
developed in the 15th Century, yet this relative
youth has not prevented cultural and religious
ideas from becoming indistinguishable such that
the religious becomes cultural and the cultural
becomes religious. Caste appears embedded
within the Sikh religion despite the fact that the
religion (or political doctrine as Guru Nanak Dev
Ji preferred to conceive it as) was born as reaction
against social inequality and difference. It appears
that cultural factors drive the caste system within
the Sikh community rather than it being part of
the fundamental Sikh religion.

In the vein of 'if you can't beat em, join em..',
Muslim communities have also joined in on the
'I'm better than you' game. This despite the fact
that many religious scholars argue that caste as a
concept is not recognised in Islam. Some
commentators suggest the caste system developed
as a result of the close contact with the Hindu
culture which predates Islam. Others suggest that
it can be linked to Hindu converts to Islam.

The system can be broadly divided in two castes:
Ashraf or oonchi zaat referring to the high caste
and Ajlaf or niichi zaat representing the lower
caste. Not forgetting of course, the Arzal or under-
caste, otherwise known as the Dalit Muslims.

The basis upon which Muslim caste systems are
developed can vary significantly. Some are rooted
in ethnic background and regional differences such
as in Pakistan. These include Sindhi, Punjabi,
Pushtun, Balouchi, Mohajir. Others are based on
religious or sectarian backgrounds, for example
Shia and Sunni. These latter two groups doing
their level best to destroy each other in various
parts of the Middle East, most notably in the
aftermath of the US led invasion of Saddam
Hussain's Iraq amd more recently evident in
conflicts in Iran and Syrai.

Bengali Muslims use the term 'Quoms' to identify
their caste system. As with the other Asian
communities mentioned earlier the high and low

quoms are characterised by a rigid social segregation with little or no inter marriage.

A casteless society?

In Britain today caste continues to cast a deep shadow, almost as inescapable as cloudy rainy days during British summers. Log onto any Asian matrimonial website (of which there are many, such as Shaadi.com and Sikhmatimonials.com) and the caste category pings out at you alongside other key filtering information such as age, occupation, education, weight and so on. In most personal profiles caste preferences are explicitly stated,be that Jatt, Brahmin, Khatri etc. Like for like is de rigueur. In others the assumption is more implicit, that is by simply stating one's personal caste background, individuals are sending out a message to potential partners that caste is a significant factor. A small minority of marriage ads state 'caste no bar', that is, for only an enlightened few is caste background irrelevant. Caste then, for most Asians, is still a key factor in selecting a lifelong marriage partner.

Matrimonial sections in Asian newspapers are less subtle in stating partner preferences. These personal ads are more likely to be placed by parents on behalf of their children (often without the latter's knowledge) and tend to follow a standard format. Matrimonial adverts in the Asian newspaper Des Pardes, typically goes something along the lines of 'we are seeking a respectable educated Jatt Sikh male for our daughter' or, 'we are seeking a suitable educated girl from a good Khatri family'. Caste then takes precedence, although one does wonder whether those who have placed the ads would rather marry their kids off to people of the same caste that are uneducated and come from disrespectful or bad families, rather than so-called respectable families whose kids are educated but of a different caste. On top of such perceived respectability there also appears to be a preference for partners that are 'tall, fair skinned and clean shaven'. The last attribute applying more to men than women.

Asian marriage bureaus or introduction agencies have also got in on the act of asserting caste differences. Dinner parties or more formal balls are a key part of their modus operandi aimed at bringing single Asians together. Upon arrival at such events, instead of being handed a glass of cheap wine, the singletons are given an identity label by the organisers. The sticky labels, typically state the persons age range such as 25 – 30 (as opposed to specific age as ironically this is deemed be too sensitive), occupation, ethnic and caste background. Thus as one walks around networking in a bid to discover one's life partner, a quick glance at your opposite numbers label will provide you with key filtering information. Thus, if Manpreet Kaur who is an Accountant of Punjabi Jatt background, aged between 30 and 35 doesn't rock your world, you can quickly move on to the

41

next id label that might meet your requirements. The initial approach is usually physical attraction, however any progression is terminated by reading the label.

The method might strike you as being crass and unsubtle, but for those weaned on the caste system this is seen as a practical and effective way of finding a marriage partner. Indeed, the labelling system does have some merits. At the very least it's a time saver. However, maybe the event organisers are missing a trick. They could add more pertinent information such as willingness to share housework; past criminal record, health record and so on. Arguably such information is more relevant than the archaic reference to an individual's caste background.

Even more primitive is the reaction of a minority of Asian people to inter caste marriages. Where such marriages do take place, albeit in the minority, the people involved can often find themselves at the centre of unwanted attention. At one level the married couple can be ostracised by their family and wider community. At the more extreme, newspaper reports have highlighted cases of threats of violence, actual violence and even the murder of one of the individuals involved, usually the female. Such sensationalist reports often run with the headline 'Honour Killing' stating that family honour and respect has been undermined by the individual concerned by marrying out of caste or marrying someone that has not been approved of by the family. One such example being the case of 20 year old Banaz Mahmod whose body was found in a suitcase in a garden in Birmingham. She was murdered by her father Mahmod Mahmod and uncle, Ari Mahmod in what police described as a honour killing. Police estimate that there may be at least 12 honour killings in the UK each year.

Conclusion

Despite claims to the contrary, it appears that a person's caste continues to be a vital consideration in the Asian community, particularly in relation to issues of marriage. Some change is taking place with an increase in mixed caste marriages and relationships, however inter caste marriages remain in the minority. Moreover, when questioned, third generation Asians in Britain are most likely to reply that 'caste doesn't matter', however the reality is that unfortunately it still does.

It is also pertinent to point out that caste systems are not peculiar to the South Asian community such that established caste systems can be found as far afield as China, Korea, Japan, Yemen and Latin America. More commonly, whilst caste systems may not exist in Western industrialised nations, another form of social hierarchy is apparent in the form of class systems, whereby

social segregation on the basis of economic factors
is the order of the day.

No BMWs

Racism and racial prejudice, unfortunately, is not the exclusive preserve of extremist groups in Britain such as the British National Party and the English Defence League. Neither is it restricted to working men club comedians such as Bernard Manning and Jim Davidson. The Asian community, like other ethnic minority groups in Britain, including Jewish, Greek and Polish communities, has its fair share of bigots. Nowhere is this bigotry more pronounced than in the arena of marriage nuptials. In Asian households across the country children have been weaned on a diet of what can be described as unrestrained racism. This is most obviously manifest in Asian children being taught from an early age that certain races are not acceptable when it comes to choosing a person to marry. The rules of unacceptability are not quite as black and white as one would expect, but reflect a complexity or pecking order of races – varying from the tolerable although not ideal variety to the 'only over my dead body' can you marry that person.

Surinder, a 25 year old female college lecturer reflected on how she was taught from a very young age that she had to marry within her race. 'My parents said I could only marry an Indian person and more specifically someone of the same ethnic background as me which is Punjabi. It was clear to me that if I married out of race I would be disowned by my immediate and extended family. I was told in no uncertain terms that I could not marry a black, Muslim or white person. My Punjabi friends had had the same experience and were told the same rules. I wasn't happy with this situation as I saw my parents as being racist, yet you sort of come to accept that this is the way things are culturally'.

Such is the level of acceptance of such cultural restrictions that among a younger generation of Punjabis in Britain it is not unusual to hear reference being made to the term 'no BMWs' when conversations turn to marriage. This acronym not referring to the popular car manufacturer which alongside Mercedes still seems to be the top of the list of Asian material possessions, rather in this context it stands for 'no Blacks, Muslims or Whites'. Successive generations of Hindus and Punjabis in Britain have been socialised by parents, aunts, uncles, community and temple elders (and often complete Asian strangers!) into marrying their own kind. Muslim and black people being considered the most taboo race, whilst white people are deemed 'not ideal, but tolerable' as one 50 year old Punjabi mother of three put it.

Caucasians are seen as being the lesser of the three evils, which is ironic in that historically a black race has never been responsible for invading India as did imperialist Britain, committing a

range of well documented atrocities in its
uninvited 90 year stay (the British outstaying its
welcome much longer than the average unexpected
Asian relative!). The British government assumed
direct control over India in 1858 taking over the
helms from the East India Company which had
laid the foundations for the 'British Raj' years
earlier (the Company was granted trading rights
in 1617 when India was under the Mughal
Empire).

Anti black and anti Muslim sentiments are not
restricted to Punjabi's, but also extend also to the
Hindu and Gujarati communities in Britain –
racial prejudice unfortunately travels well.
Deepak, a 28 year old Gujarati accountant
commented 'my parents said I could marry anyone
I wanted as long as they weren't black or Muslim.
They would prefer me to marry a Gujarati girl but
said they would accept a Hindu or Sikh girl.' It is
not uncommon to hear Asian parents start
sentences with the immortal words '...you can
marry anyone you want as long as they are....',
ringing an unfortunate similarity to the infamous
quote attributed to the great American car
manufacturer Henry Ford: '....you can have the car
in any colour so long as its black...'. Freedom of
choice in the Asian culture is as rare as that in a
North Korean leadership election.

When Neena, a 38 year old Hindu-Punjabi finance
clerk informed her parents that she had met
someone she wanted to marry, her parents

response was simple and short: 'As long he is not black or Muslim we do not mind who you marry.' Fortunately for Neena, her partner was a 29 year old Gujarati male. She thought her parents would have a problem with the age difference as well as the ethnic difference, however she concluded: 'I think my parents were just desperate to see me married off at my age!' It is unusual for an Asian woman of 38 years to be single in the Asian community, indeed if a woman is not by married by 30 she is considered over the hill and destined to be on the shelf for eternity. She becomes less attractive as a viable marriage proposition – as marketable as selling sand in the Sahara desert. Asian aunties will cast furtive glances at social events at such women, often making negative comments suggesting 'something is wrong with the girl' or 'she must have a white boyfriend'. As if being a female, Asian, over 30 and single is a dire affliction akin to leprosy – incurable and socially unacceptable.

Despite the issue of age, race continues to play a dominant role. Just as Sikh and Hindu children are warned they cannot marry Muslims or black people, the reverse is true also. Muslim children are also taught that they cannot marry a non-Muslim. Isma, a successful 29 year old single barrister reflected: 'My parents have given me a three line whip – I cannot marry a non Muslim, it's as simple as that. Sikhs and Hindus are definitely not allowed, they are seen to have the worst habits including drinking alcohol and eating

pork. This is a real pity as many of my male
friends are Sikhs and Hindus who are more liberal
minded than Muslim males so would probably
make better partners. However, my parents would
disown me if I married a non – Muslim, so it's not
an option unfortunately.'

Historical context

Various explanations can be identified to help us
understand such racial intolerance. These tend to
be based on cultural, historical and/or political
factors, depending on which one suits at the time.
The more deep seated historical prejudices
between Hindus and Muslims can be understood
against the backdrop of Mughal invasions of India
which can be dated back to medieval times. The
Turko - Muslim invasion of India in 1032
essentially laid the foundations of racial conflict
which continues today, however Islamic influence
in India can be traced back to the seventh century
with the impact of Arab traders and the first wave
of settlers. Going further back in time, historians
have identified ships bearing Muslim travellers on
the Indian coast as early as 630 AD.

Following the 11th Century invasion, Muhammed
of Ghor effectively laid the foundations of the
Mughal empire in India in the 12th Century,
leading to the creation of the Dehli Sultanate.
However, the classic period of the Mughal Empire
starts with the rise of Jalaluddin Mohammed,
more commonly known as Akbar the Great, in

1556. Akbar's period of rule has been characterised by tolerance (this of course, is a relative concept, as Akbar did oversee one or two massacres!) of the conquered Hindu majority, such that the latter were not forced to obey Islamic laws. Akbar encouraged intermarriage and married a Hindu princess, although how special she was amongst his several thousand other wives could be debated! He developed the so called hybrid religion of 'God-ism' which mixed Islamic, Hindu, Christian and Buddhist teachings and awarded Hindu's some of the highest ranks in government. This period tends to be underplayed by those wishing to perpetuate the differences between Hindus and Muslims, particularly when it comes to issues of marriage.

Such tolerance and inclusiveness was not encouraged so wholeheartedly by Akbar's son and successor, Emperor Jahangir. In putting down various rebellions against the government, he was responsible for the destruction of Hindu temples and the torture to death of Guru Arjun, the fifth Guru of Sikhs. Having said that, it is contended that Jahangir enjoyed friendly relations with Guru Arjun's son and successor, Guru Hargobind. Jahangir himself was replaced by Shah Jahan, famous for commissioning the Taj Mahal (1630 – 1653). The last great Mughal Emperor was Aurangzeb, who was not as liberal, to say the least, as his predecessors. The fact that he came to power after imprisoning his father and having his brother killed, gives you some indication of his mindset. He no longer allowed the Hindu community to live under their own laws and customs, but imposed Sharia law and taxes on non-Muslims. He oversaw the destruction of thousands of Hindu temples and shrines, as well as pushing forward the policy of conversion. A body of graphic evidence exists highlighting the punishments afforded those who refused to convert to Islam from the most imaginative examples of torture to the more bog standard public beheadings.

The growth of Sikhism and the formation of Khalsa in 1699 is in part a reaction to Mughal rule and the policies of conversion by the sword. Indeed, Augrangzeb is credited with ordering the execution of the 9th Sikh Guru, Tegh Bahadur in 1675 and subsequently the murder of four sons of the 10th Guru, Gobind Rai. Such historical episodes continue to fuel the antagonisms between Sikhs, Hindus and Muslims in Britain today and perhaps shape the reluctance towards intermarriage in the Asian community. Muslim interpretations of this period of history would no doubt point to the atrocities committed by Hindus and Sikhs.

Fast forwarding, the flame of Mughal rule was finally put out by the British in 1857, with the establishment of British India in 1858 following the brutal suppression of the Indian revolt of 1857-58. The British crown, under Queen Victoria, assumed the Mughal mantle for the next ninety years up to India's independence in 1947. A mass of literature both contemporary and historical already exists, variously singing the praises of British imperialist rule or highlighting its worst excesses. For example, it cannot be denied that major improvements in transport and communications took place during British rule. Railways, roads, bridges and telegraph links were built on a grand scale. By 1920 India had the fourth largest railway network in the world. The introduction of new technologies associated with industrialization saw output in manufacturing and agriculture increase significantly.

On the other hand, it has been argued that such progress was paid for by Indians in the form of blood, sweat, tears and taxation. India also experienced some of its worst famines during this period in which millions are said to have died due to poor administration by the British and the fact that food grains were being produced for export markets rather than the poor starving Indians. There are countless examples of oppressive measures used by the British to control the so called 'natives' who were seen as second class citizens. This attitude perhaps epitomised by Viceroy General Mayo (1869–72) when he commented: "....we are engaged in the work of governing an inferior race..." One notable example of the British desire to control its subjects being the massacre at the Jallianwallah Garden in Amritsar in 1919. General Dyer gave the order for 2000 rounds to be fired, without warning, on a unarmed crowd of around 10,000 men, women and children at a peaceful albeit prohibited demonstration. It is estimated that 379 people were killed and up to 1200 wounded for whom medical attention was restricted.

It is perhaps not surprising then that under the British Raj personal relationships between Indians and the British were discouraged and inter marriages rare. However, there is some irony, considering the historical context, in the fact that in contemporary Britain, relationships and marriage between Asians and whites tend to be more acceptable than those between the different Asian ethnic groups themselves, such as Hindus and Muslims. Some would argue that this very issue can be related to the last great act of treachery the British imposed on India resulting in its vivisection. It has been argued that the British actively cultivated communal violence in India between Hindus, Sikhs and Muslims (which continues today) in its policy of 'divide and rule' culminating in the act of partition.

The events of India's more recent history have further embedded if not increased racial bigotry between Hindus, Sikhs and Muslims in Britain such that inter-racial marriage continues to be a taboo subject. The British failure to effectively manage partition between India and the newly formed Pakistan in 1947 essentially cemented the conflict between the two countries and the various ethnic groups involved. Partition remains the single largest uprooting of people in modern history as between 12 to 14 million people left their homes to cross the new border and set up home again. Such a movement of people was not by choice but rather under fear or threat of attack from the respective ethnic majority, be that Indian or Pakistani. Partition was accompanied by an unparalleled level of communal violence characterised by the mass genocide of men, women and children on both sides of the border. The estimates of how many people died vary enormously from 500,000 to 1.5 million. Such events, unsurprisingly, have left deep scars on the Hindu, Sikh and Muslim communities affected and continue to shape the current relations of mistrust and intolerance.

Mohammed Ali Jinnah's insistence on the creation of a separate Pakistani state was largely a reflection of a feeling of persecution amongst Muslims in India. That is the fear of being a minority against the Hindu majority, which in turn reflects deep rooted antagonisms between the two groups based on religious differences. Jinnah perhaps didn't help matters when he stated Muslims could not trust the 'crafty Hindus'. This has resulted in paranoia between the two countries characterised but mutual suspicion, mistrust and the constant fear of attack, not dissimilar to the Arab – Israeli situation.

More recent history

Pakistan has consistently argued that since its independence on August 14th 1947, India has been engaged in a concerted attempt to crush the newly formed Pakistani state. Pakistanis refer to the Arthashastra as 'proof' of India's government being engaged in activities of subversion, espionage and deceit. India, unsurprisingly has denied any such involvement and its attempts to reassure Pakistan that it accepts its statehood has fallen on deaf ears. Such mutual suspicion and fear has been further fuelled by a number of wars between the two countries. Pakistan was defeated in the 1965 Kashmir war. The 1971 war which resulted in the loss of East Pakistan and the subsequent creation of Bangladesh added insult to injury. Relations between the two countries took a further setback during the 1999 Kargil war.

Despite attempts at diplomacy both sides remain hostile to each other and this is most obviously manifest in the continuing Kashmiri conflict. Old accusations continue to fly across the mutual border. Indian nationalists accuse maulvis (Islamic teachers) in Pakistan of breeding and inciting anti – Indian feelings thus promoting hatred and suspicion. At the more extreme end, Hindu nationalists focus on those aspects of Islamic teachings that portray a world divided between believers and unbelievers, whereby the former are obliged to convert the latter. More radical Indian commentators point to the actions of Islamic Jihadist's who they argue seek not only the liberation of Muslims in Kashmir but also the liberation of all Muslims in India. There are approximately 151 million Muslims in India, constituting just over 13% of the population according to the 2001 Census. Conversely, Pakistanis accuse India of wanting to 'undo Pakistan' again reflecting the concerns of a relatively newly formed state. Such insecurity being advanced by India's growing economic and military superiority. However, there is also a feeling amongst Pakistanis that partition was imperfectly carried out such that the issue of Muslims in India still needs to be resolved.

Contemporary picture

Contemporary Indo-Pak relations continue to be frosty, to say the least. There is a recurrent prospect of nuclear conflict between the two states particularly over Kashmir. The rise of Islamic extremism in Pakistan most recently manifesting itself in the 2008 and 2011 Mumbai bombings has been mirrored by the rise of Hindu nationalism in the form of political parties such as the BJP and RSS promoting an extremist Hindutva agenda in India. The latter groups have been accused of being instrumental in the destruction of the Muslim mosque in Ayodhya (1992) and the subsequent inter – racial communal violence in India between Hindus and Muslims which left 2000 people dead. In Gujarat in 2002, communal violence again erupted resulting in more deaths of both Hindus and Muslims.

Unfortunately, conflict and prejudice travels well. Relationships between the different Asian communities in Britain continue to be characterised by prejudice, mistrust and in some cases violence. Conflict between Sikhs and Muslims in areas such as Derby, Birmingham and Southall tend to be a recurrent theme. Hindus and Sikhs often perceive Islam as a proselytising religion such that Islam seeks converts. Such views being reinforced by cases of anti –Sikh leaflets being distributed encouraging young Muslim males to take Sikh girls out on dates in a bid to convert them to Islam. Such girls are described as 'easy prey' as girls are seen to 'like a drink'. Despite the fact that such instances are in the minority they fuel the tension and distrust between the different communities and provide a platform for some to continue the campaign for marrying from within one's own community.

Apart from the historical context, cultural arguments are often put forward to justify intra rather than inter marriage. Amar, a 30 year old Hindu Doctor commented: "I don't think the mixing of cultures is a good idea, it just leads to cultural dilution. I don't want my kids to be confused about who they are and what their culture is, that's why I will only marry a Hindu girl." Safina, a 21 year old Muslim student reinforced this view: "My religion and my culture is very important to me. I will only marry someone who shares the same beliefs and culture. I think it's important not only to protect what we have but to pass it onto to our future children so that our cultural traditions will continue. I am not anti any other race; I just think we need to protect our different ways of life".

Vaneet, a 31 year old single Hindu Dentist took a less tolerant approach stating: 'I just don't approve of mixed marriages. It leads to confusion for children in developing their identities. For example, at a recent wedding I attended the photographer was getting close family members together for a group photograph. My niece, who is 8 years old and of mixed parentage, half Indian and half German, started to move out of the photo. I asked her why and she said that she didn't think she was part of the family as she was a different colour. My heart sank. I don't think children should have to experience such difficulties'.

Those who have embarked on mixed race marriages have had to navigate a range of issues and barriers. Michael, a non practising Christian Doctor of Afro Caribbean descent had to undergo a conversion ceremony before he could marry his childhood sweetheart, Manaza, a Muslim dentist. He reflected: 'Manaza's parents would not accept the marriage unless I converted to Islam. This meant being circumcised and changing my name to Mohammed. It was a tough experience and I had many sleepless nights deciding whether it was the right thing to do, yet things have worked okay and we now have two beautiful daughters'.

Others such as Sunita (a 27 year old Hindu GP from Leicester) have not had such positive experiences: 'I married the man I feel in love with at university. For me the fact that he was white was incidental. We have lots in common, share the same interests and we both happen to be Doctors. I knew deep down that my parents would have, in an ideal world, liked to see me marry a Hindu person, so I guessed they might have been a little disappointed when I informed them of my plans to marry David. But I wasn't at all prepared for their response, or rather my fathers. He was totally against the marriage and talked of issues of family respect and so on and promised that he would not attend the marriage if it went ahead. At the time I thought he would come round to the idea, as we had had a very loving positive father – daughter relationship. Unfortunately he didn't attend the wedding and although now, years later, we have a relationship of sorts, it is not what it used to be.'

Mixed race marriages

Britain has one of the fastest growing mixed race populations in the world reflected in the high number of inter – ethnic relationships and marriages. According to the 2001 Census 10% of Asian women were opting for a white partner, whilst the figure was around 20% for Asian men.

Whilst it seems that most Asian women are marrying 'their own' the 10% figure represents a growing minority. Praveen, a 32 year old Hindu public relations manager who has married a white partner argues that a growing number of Asian women in Britain 'prefer to marry white because English men are more tolerant and less patriarchal. I think there is a common perception amongst a number of Asian women that most Asian men have traditional views as to how their wife should act and behave. The number of times I have heard Asian women complain as to how their partner changed once they got married from being supposedly liberal to suddenly 'Indian traditional'.'

Sukhjit, a 28 year old Punjabi medical representative, who now lives with a white partner after divorcing a Punjabi boy commented: 'The day after we got married he changed. He started telling me how to dress and expected me to do all the cooking and cleaning, telling me how this has worked for his mom and dad and so it was good enough for him. English white guys are more liberal and seem to understand the term equality. I don't ever plan to have a relationship with an Asian guy again'.

Such views, however strong, appear to be in the minority as 9 out of ten Asian women are opting for Asian partners. Moreover, according to the last Census, inter-ethnic marriages account for only two per cent (around 219,000) of all marriages in Britain. Of this 219,000, 11% were made up of white and Indian partners. People from South Asian backgrounds were least likely of the ethnic minority groups in Britain to marry outside of their own race. Pakistanis and Bangladeshis have the lowest rates of inter-marriage – 3% and 4% respectively.

Such statistics highlight the fact that inter-ethnic marriages continue to be a minority affair and thus do not constitute such a great threat to ethnic cultures as some may like us to believe. However, media reports of so-called 'honour killings' in the Asian community highlight the fact that for some inter-ethnic marriages are still unacceptable. The perpetrators of such killings are often motivated by the fact that the victim had married, intended to marry or merely had a relationship with someone outside of the culture and thus bought what was perceived 'shame' on the family otherwise referred to as a loss of izzat (respect) in the community. Indeed, supporters of such heinous crimes suggest that honour killings send a clear message to others in the community that marrying out of race is unacceptable and will not be tolerated. It is estimated that around 10,000 honour killings take place each year in India compared with up to a dozen women in the UK from almost exclusively Asian or Middle Eastern families of which two-thirds are Muslim. However, Britain has seen a rise in honour-related crime with around 3000 incidents in 2010 including house arrests and other parental punishments.

Some high profile cases in the UK include that of Gurmeet Singh Ubhi, a Sikh man who, in February 2011, was found guilty of the murder of his 24 year-old daughter, Amrit Kaur Ubhi in 2010. Mr. Ubhi was found to have murdered his daughter because he disapproved of her being 'too westernised' and he also disapproved of the fact that she was dating a non-Sikh man. This case was strikingly similar to that of the parents of Shafilea Ahmed, from Warrington, Cheshire, who were convicted in 2012 of murdering their daughter in 2003. The 17-year-old was suffocated because she had become 'too westernised' and refused to participate in a forced marriage in Pakistan. Whilst such cases are still in the extreme minority it appears that honour killings are not as reviled as one may expect, for example, a 2006 BBC poll for the Asian network in the UK found that one in ten of the 500 young Asians polled said that they could condone the killing of someone who dishonored their family. More recently (2013), leaders of caste councils in India made a plea to the Supreme Court for greater understanding of those who kill their children for 'honour'.

It appears that for some women in the UK insisting on marrying a man they love can result in a very heavy price being paid.

More recent data from the 2011 Census suggest a trend of increased mixed marriages amongst all ethnic groups in the UK, however within the Asian ethnic minorities that change is less pronounced. Marriages between Asians and black African and Afro-Caribbean people are still in the extreme minority as are marriages between Muslims (of Pakistani and Bangladeshi origin) and Hindus; and Muslims and Punjabi Sikhs. Such marriage types continue to be culturally taboo.

Shady.com

Open up an Asian wedding invitation card and invariably you will come across a romanticised statement which goes something along the lines of: **'Marriages are made in heaven and celebrated on earth'.** Well, this no longer seems appropriate in the modern digital internet age. There has been an explosion of Asian marriage sites on the internet over the last decade including sites such as Shaadi.com, Sikhmatrimonials.com, singlemuslim.com and SimplyMarry.com to name but a few. Such sites have captured a growing new market of Asians of all ethnic backgrounds eager to find their own life partner and essentially 'arrange their own marriage'. No longer are the new generation of Asians reliant on divine intervention or parents, aunts and uncles to introduce them to so-called 'potentials'. Marriages are less likely to be made in heaven but rather on the information super highway.

It does appear that parents are now taking a back seat in the marriage process, whereas in the past they played a central role in selecting their children's life partner. However, whilst third generation British Asians may be taking more control over the process they still appear to have held on to some of the traditions and aspirations of their parents in their attempt to navigate a middle way. That is, the criteria adopted by parents in selecting potential marriage partners are often mirrored by the choices their children are now making. This is most obvious in the fact that those putting adverts on marriage sites tend to clearly state that they are seeking a partner from a particular ethnic group, caste, language, religion, age range and so on. For example, Gurpreet (a solicitor from London) states that she is a Punjabi speaking Jat Sikh girl of 30 years of age looking for a Jat Sikh professional, who is preferably clean shaven (as opposed to having a turban and beard) between 30 and 35 years of age and at least 5 feet 8 inches – hence hairy short people need not respond. The sites themselves do what they can to make this process as easy as possible, for example, Asiancommunity.net promotes itself by stating the following:

'To make your search for a soul mate easier, we have separated potential partners by religion and caste. So why wait, the love of your life may only be one click away.'

Safraz Manzoor in a wittily entitled article for the Guardian in 2009, 'Love at First Site', highlights the fact that despite young Asians being more in control of finding their marriage partner they still conform to their parent's wishes. Manzoor comments: "In practice, they are still imprisoned by the idea that finding an ideal partner is about creed and career rather than chemistry." Indeed, it does appear that factors such as personality and physical attractiveness tend to be relegated in favour of the more important issues of religion, caste and occupation. Hina, an attractive, slim 28 year old teacher from Nottingham was quite candid in stating 'I'm not really that bothered about looks and personality as much as I am about whether he is from the right ethnic background and he comes from a respectable family. Marriage is about learning to love and other issues are more important.' When I suggest that such views are a tad old fashioned and that maybe she sounds like a pair of traditional Indian parents, she responded, 'I guess you're right. I hadn't really thought of it that way. I do remember when I was in my early twenties and my parents and various aunts and uncles who would try to introduce me to people by showing me photographs of men and I would often say oh he's ugly. They would then say that looks didn't matter – perhaps I have changed.'

So called 'Aunties' as match-makers are increasingly being replaced by Asian matrimonial sites which allow users to conduct searches based on age; occupation; marital status (divorced; never married), location etc like any other dating or matchmaking site, however what makes these marriage sites more interesting, or alarming, is the levels of specificity that are stated. For example, Amina from Wolverhampton has stated that she is looking for a 'moderate professional Muslim, preferably in Medicine or Law and of Sindhi origins. He should have a fair complexion and must come from a good family'. The potential suitor for Amina also needs to be a vegetarian and she will only consider men from the UK, Canada or USA. She probably forgot to state that he should also know how to create world peace and solve the problem of poverty.

It is worth pointing out that the emphasis on occupation and associated wealth is not restricted to Asians. If you pick up any glossy Western European magazine you will invariably see very beautiful tall model type women on the arms of short unattractive men who just happen to be rich. However, the distinguishing factor on the marriage sites is the primary focus on religion, ethnicity and caste. Having said that, Suki (a 32 year old Punjabi accountant from Manchester) admitted that whilst she was able to tick the boxes in terms of caste, religion, personality and physical attractiveness, the occupation box was the deal breaker for her: 'I met a very handsome Bollywood star type looking man from Birmingham who was really lovely and we got on really well, but he was a Prison Warden and I wanted someone more professional. We had a fling but it didn't go any further than that unfortunately.' Fahmida (a 30 year old Doctor from Bradford) is a little more blunt in commenting 'I'm not really bothered about chemistry or looks as long as he is an educated Pakistani professional with a good job. We'll learn to love each other over time just like our parents did.'

Despite the fact the issues of ethnicity, occupation and caste tend to take precedence over looks or physical attractiveness, the latter is still important, particularly for men. Indeed, all the matrimonial sites encourage the uploading of personal images to online profiles as these are more likely to generate more responses but they can also highlight potential problems with such sites. Aryan, a 34 year old Punjabi Doctor from Coventry learnt at significant personal financial and emotional cost that all is not what it seems on the information superhighway. He recalls how he had contacted a potential girl on a Sikh matrimonial site based primarily on her photograph. He reflects 'Yes, I'll admit that I saw the photograph first and then read her profile. I thought she looked beautiful – that was a big attraction for me. Anyway, I made contact and we exchanged a number of emails and phone calls. To cut a longish story short I decided to go and see her despite the fact that she was based in India. I organised a short three day trip due to work commitments and as soon as I landed after dropping my suitcase at the hotel, I went straight to our agreed meeting point in a pizza place in central Delhi. As soon as I walked in I saw her and as I neared her table I noticed how different she looked to her photograph. As I sat down I realised that she had a very severe skin condition on the left hand side of her face. During the course of our brief conversation it dawned on me that all her photographs on the marriage site were of her right side profile. Needless to say we didn't meet again....'

Aryan's experience is not an isolated one with different degrees of deception being commonplace on matrimonial sites. More minor deception may include some girls stating that they 'love to cook' when they don't. Others may list a whole host of hobbies including mountain climbing; paragliding; swimming when they haven't actually done of any these. Some people have put up fake profile pictures using images of models or actors and actresses to help ensure responses. Others have used pictures of friends or other family members to help ensure an initial response. For example, Anil, a Hindu Punjabi IT Consultant from Watford, arranged to meet a girl in London based on a couple of emails and liking the look of her photographs. When they met he immediately realised she wasn't the person in the photographs. When she was challenged on this she reluctantly admitted that she had used her younger sister's photos because she was prettier. Anil commented, 'she didn't appear particularly embarrassed and felt that it shouldn't matter too much as they could just get to know each other. I made a quick exit and removed my profile from the site.'

Such deception is not restricted to people trying to find a life partner but also people (mostly men) pretending to be single when they may be married or in a relationship using the sites to find potential sexual partners. A married man from Bradford who, unsurprisingly, wants to remain anonymous candidly admitted to using the shaadi.com website to meet girls and 'have some fun'. He said 'I do feel a little bad about lying and being married but I've met a lot of girls on the site that are more up for dating rather than settling down. I can keep the messing around undercover as the girls usually don't let their parents know who they are meeting unless it gets serious. I usually end a relationship before it gets that far. It's probably why the site is called shady.com – everyone's up to no good!'

Fatima a 29 year old teacher from the West Midlands stopped using the marriage sites when she found that most of the men she met put up photographs of themselves when they were a lot younger. She said 'I can't remember the number of men I met who put photographs of themselves when they were a lot younger and they had hair and were thinner. Overweight and baldness is not a look I go for. I'm sure I've also met a couple of men who are already married. It seems my options are very limited. I'm thinking of asking my parents to help.' Shaykh Jamil, an Islamic scholar who set up a family counselling service called Unity Family Services, said: "There are many well-educated women up and down the country who want to get married but are not finding the right match. There is an acute shortage of suitable male options and the ones who are available are getting married from back home.

Jamil goes further and argues that as many Asian women in Scotland can't find a partner in Britain they reluctantly have to bring someone over from South Asia and that can lead to problems. The men coming over tend to have a different mentality and different expectations. For example, the men may have more traditional ways of living including women staying at home and performing the dutiful housewife role. Amina is a 38-year-old single woman from Glasgow. She is currently unemployed, but worked in the legal sector before retraining with a degree in finance, commented on how most of the men on the sites from Pakistan seemed more interested in coming over to live in Britain rather than getting married. She said 'I got the impression that they weren't interested in me as much as they were in getting a visa to stay in the UK.'

Internet searches, chat room and twitter accounts provide a further picture of the problems associated with Asian matrimonial sites. One disgruntled customer commented on twitter that 'shaadi.com is a scam. They have tons of fake profiles with pictures of pretty girls. The websites work in a devious way. They want to keep your interest in the website for as long as they can. As soon as you cancel your account or it expires you will be bombarded with acceptances from profiles you have sent an interest to months ago.'

Another customer from the UK noted: 'most of the fake profiles you will come across are from the

USA. Another sign you should look out for is profiles with just one image and these images are usually small in size. However she does go on to reflect that '....in their defence, I have met a few good people, let's say for every 20 fake profiles you will come across one real person.'

At the more extreme end of deception one unfortunate customer has sent out a warning to others on the internet after she was scammed of almost £30,000. 'Beware of this man. He has many profiles on Shaadi with different photos. His profiles are allalone_1960, allalone_10 (SH01605488) and SH38824573. He said he is a Muslim, I am also a Muslim. He claimed he prayed 5 times a day and goes to the mosque regularly. I was vulnerable when I answered his profile (I had just lost my child) and he preyed on my emotions. He pretended he had 2 sons schooling in England and that he is a widow and was experiencing financial problems. I later discovered this was all lies. He is a SCAM. Ladies look out.....'

Another popular story of deception that regularly appears on internet chatrooms is that of a rather disgruntled Indian male who arranged to meet a potential female partner via a matrimonial site. On meeting said female he soon realised that she was really a he! The so-called female had not had a sex change operation but was apparently 'mid-transition'. Needless to say the couple did not end up walking hand in hand into a romantic sunset.

Some of have suggested that this story is more urban myth than reality.

Do marriage sites work?

Despite the problems associated with the plethora of Asian marriage sites it appears that their popularity has not diminished, such that those seeking love and marriage online is a growing phenomenon. An internet search of such sites will quickly reveal personal testimonies including photographs and video footage of real weddings of Asian couples who have met online. Indeed, for those who do not have the time or inclination to try conventional routes of meeting their life partner via family weddings, socialising with friends, parties etc., the internet has been a welcome revelation. For some, these sites also provide a welcome alternative to Asian speed dating events or Desi padlock and key singles nights.

The internet is a very powerful, accessible and increasingly socially acceptable way to meet and marry. Marriage sites also offer individuals greater choice and control, rather than having to rely on matchmaking Asian Aunties. The internet opens up a much wider global pool of potential partners from Southampton to Sydney. Indeed non Asians are also using the sites such as John from Dorset who states on his profile: 'I'm a Englishman of 51, an ex-serviceman of 22 years and live in the south of England and I find Indian Pakistani and Chinese Woman a cut above English woman.'

Shaadi.com, the Indian based site founded by Anupam Mittal and People Group in 1997, is described as the world's largest matrimonial service. Shaadi.com claims to have the highest number of users and successful matches (822,073 as of 2009 and over 1.3 million as of 2011). It has got competition from the likes of BharatMatrimony.com and Jeevansathi.com but shaadi.com continues to be the leader of the pack. The website claims that the service has touched the lives of over 20 million people globally and has helped over 2 million people find their matches. Anupam Mittal, who incidentally is still a bachelor at 40, not the greatest advert for a matrimonial site, argues that there has been a sea change in attitudes such that looking online for love is no longer a sign of desperation but enables people to exercise greater choice. However, he does say that 'parental blessing' is still a key factor in the decision making process.

Shaadi.com has not rested on its laurels and continues to expand its matrimonial business. In the offline space, 2004 saw the launch of Shaadi.com Centers which are essentially a network of retail outlets across India that offer a range of matrimonial related services including wedding planning and advice for both parents and potential spouses. It has recently collaborated with Vodafone and produced a marriage app. Another interesting development is SecondShaadi.com which the creators claim is the 'No.1 matrimonial site for Indians looking for a second marriage. So, whether you are divorced or widowed, give us a try and start a new life!' This latter initiative is positive in that the stigma traditionally associated with divorcees in the Asian community is waning such that divorce is no longer seen as a taboo topic. The flip side is that divorce rates are increasing amongst Asians, almost as fast as current inflation rates. Nonetheless, matrimonial sites continue to be big business with some estimates of shaadi.com being worth around 1.5 billion rupees.

Conclusion

Going online may be easier than going to parents and each marriage site can boast successful couplings, however there is a trend developing whereby 3rd generation Asians are returning to the tried and tested traditional methods of parental involvement. Those who have dipped their toes in the murky pool of internet marriage sites where it is difficult to know the true intentions of the person tapping into your inbox have sought parental help.

After a number of disappointing dates via shaadi.com, Seema has now left the online scene commenting 'I know it sounds a bit of a cop out but

I have had too many disasters via the marriage sites and have told my parents to find me someone. At the end of the day I trust my parents and I know they want the best for me, whereas the internet is very hit and miss. I will continue to be open to finding someone myself but it hasn't worked so far...'.

On the other hand, some parents have actually created profiles on behalf of their respective children (one would hope with the consent of their loved ones, however it would not be surprising if this wasn't the case). In such instances parents have acted as a filtering mechanism in selecting potential suitors.

Epilogue

Within the space of the last decade or so there has been a sea change in the cultural habits of the Asian community in Great Britain in terms of marriage. The traditional arranged marriage model, whilst not quite disappearing, appears to increasingly apply to a small minority of die hards. That is, some traditionalists still feel that as parents it is their duty to arrange the marriages of their children, with or without the latter's consent. In India, it is estimated that approximately 90% of marriages are still arranged in the traditional sense with less than 2% ending in divorce. At face value the low divorce rate is a great advert for the success of arranged marriages. However, the divorce statistics may hide the number of unhappy or empty shell marriages that may exist. That is, due to family and cultural pressures, couples are deterred from getting divorced. Divorce still having a significant stigma attached to it within the Asian diaspora.

Nevertheless, 3rd and 4th generation Asians are striking out on their own. This is evident in the increase of Asian matrimonial sites; the growing popularity of so-called 'love marriages'; and the growing trend of mixed marriages, such as British Indians marrying British Caucasians. This generation is less willing to follow in the footsteps of their parents and indeed parents may be encouraging their children to 'find their own' partner. Either the way the shift away from traditional cultural habits in relation to marriage is a growing phenomenon. The younger generations have effectively assimilated into Western ideals of choice and love when it comes to marriage. On the other hand, it appears that the old adage that 'the fruit doesn't fall far from the tree' still holds true. That is, whilst the younger generation Asians may be arranging their own marriages, they still tend to follow the criteria that their parents would have preferred in terms of marrying someone with the same ethnic, religious, caste and cultural background.

It is also worth mentioning the middle way that some Asians are navigating, that is, the 'semi-arranged marriage'. This is where parents are actively involved in identifying 'potential suitors' for their loved ones and thus acting as a sort of introduction agency. Parents will pass on details and phone numbers to their children and encourage them to meet and date and work out compatibility themselves. In this instance, parents will emphasize to their children that they can make their own choices in terms of marriage. Not dissimilar to friends arranging blind dates for one another. The big difference is that parents will have a particular set of criteria as discussed earlier in this book.

It is too early to judge whether arranging your own marriage or semi arranged marriages will be as, or more successful than traditional arranged marriages. One thing is for certain, marriage isn't easy, regardless of the form in which it may occur.